Selected Poems of Thoma

CW01425484

A Critical Study Guide

Thomas Hardy 1840-1928

Thomas Hardy, the son of a Dorset mason, worked as an architect for many years yet always wanted to be a writer. His first novel, published in 1871, was not well-received by the public, but his next book, *Under the Greenwood Tree* (1872), did much better. Hardy eventually published many novels, including *Far from the Madding Crowd* and The *Mayor of Casterbridge*, but his work proved controversial and critics savagely condemned his last two works: *Jude the Obscure* and *Tess of the d'Urbervilles*. Yet Hardy no longer needed to write prose fiction for a living - the royalties from his existing work gave him more than enough security. He had always preferred poetry - and believed that he was better as a writer in this form. He wrote verse throughout his life, but did not publish a volume until *Wessex Poems and Other Verses* (for which he did his own illustrations) appeared in 1898. Hardy certainly made up for lost time, eventually publishing 947 poems (some of which are hard to date as they appear in different periodicals).

Thomas Hardy was married twice - his first marriage, long and mostly unhappy, was to Emma Gifford. In 1870, while on an architectural mission to restore a parish church in Cornwall, Hardy met and fell in love with Emma, whom he married in 1874. Although they later became estranged, her death in November 1912 had a traumatic effect on him. After her death, Hardy made a trip to Cornwall to revisit places linked with their courtship, and his Poems 1912–13 reflect upon her death. In 1914, Hardy married his secretary Florence Emily Dugdale, who was 39 years his junior and later became his biographer. However, he remained preoccupied with his first wife's death and tried to overcome his remorse by writing poetry. Hardy died in 1928, aged 87. He had asked to be laid beside Emma, but his body was buried in Poet's Corner in Westminster Abbey. Only his heart was placed in Emma's grave - or was it? There is a curious story that his housekeeper placed the heart on the kitchen table, where his sister's cat seized it, and ran off into the nearby woods. In this version of events, a pig's heart was duly buried beside Emma.

Critics on Hardy's Poetry

The key to Hardy's verse is authenticity. He was seized by a particular impulse – an immediate or recollected emotion combined with a particular rhythm – and would override ordinary proprieties of speech in his intense concern for faithfulness to it. P. N. Furbank

Many critics of Hardy's poetry have found themselves in the uncomfortable and ultimately preposterous position of applauding him for his clumsiness. Donald Davie

Insisting that his writing did not offer a philosophy of life, Hardy claims that each poem was an 'impression', intensely subjective and evanescent. Geoffrey Harvey

Hardy's poetry is pre-eminently about ways of seeing. This is evident in the numerous angles of vision he employs in so many poems. Sometimes it involves creating a picture, as in 'Snow in the Suburbs', which allows the eye to follow the cascading snow set off by a sparrow alighting on a tree; or it employs the camera effect, as in 'On the Departure Platform', which tracks the gradually diminishing form and disappearance of a muslin-gowned girl among those boarding the train. However, Hardy is also a poet of social observation. His humanistic sympathies emerge in a variety of poems drawing upon his experience of both Dorset and London. Geoffrey Harvey

Most of Hardy's poems, such as Neutral Tones and A Broken Appointment, deal with themes of disappointment in love and life (which were also prominent themes in his novels), and mankind's long struggle against indifference to human suffering. F.R. Leavis

If one says that he seems to have no sensitiveness for words, one recognizes at the same time that he has made a style out of stylelessness. There is something extremely personal about the gauche, unshrinking mismarriages – group-mismarriages – of his diction, in which, with naif aplomb, he takes as they come the romantic -poetical, the prosaic banal, the stilted literary, the colloquial, the archaistic, the erudite, the technical, the dialect word, the brand-new Hardy coinage. F. R. Leavis

Hardy's poems start immediately out of his own remembered past and are particular evocations of utter loss, the blindness of chance, the poignancy of love and its helplessness and the cruelty of time. F. R. Leavis

At the Word 'Farewell'   Publ. 1917

She looked like a bird from a cloud

On the clammy lawn,

Moving alone, bare-browed

In the dim of dawn.

The candles alight in the room

For my parting meal

Made all things withoutdoors loom

Strange, ghostly, unreal.

The hour itself was a ghost,

And it seemed to me then

As of chances the chance furthermost

I should see her again.

I beheld not where all was so fleet

That a Plan of the past

Which had ruled us from birthtime to meet

Was in working at last:

No prelude did I there perceive

To a drama at all,

Or foreshadow what fortune might weave

From beginnings so small;

But I rose as if quicked by a spur

I was bound to obey,

And stepped through the casement to her

Still alone in the gray.

'I am leaving you...Farewell!' I said,

As I followed her on

By an alley bare boughs overspread;

'I soon must be gone!'

Even then the scale might have been turned

Against love by a feather,

- But crimson one cheek of hers burned

When we came in together.

Commentary

The setting for the enigmatic *At the Word 'Farewell'* is a haunted, muted morning with a figure walking outside. The air was so grey that it appears like time and the hour itself is a ghost. In the first stanza Hardy opens with a simile and the bird on a clammy lawn implies that she is attractive, possibly heavenly, but momentarily earthbound. For some critics Hardy is describing the memory of his wife Emma, who died in November in 1912, and the authorial intention is to highlight the two lovers' destiny and to emphasize Hardy's desperation to be with her. The mood conveys both devotion and sorrow, while the major ideas are of hope and fate. Hardy uses pathetic fallacy when he says 'dim of dawn'. 'Dawn' implies a new beginning, but 'dim' undermines the joyful connotations of morning.

In stanza two Hardy shows that from 'birthtime' they were destined to meet. In the phrase, 'bound to obey', Hardy creates an image of attachment; the word 'bound' conveys that wherever the woman goes, the narrator is bound to follow. 'Obey' denotes not being given a choice which is exactly how the narrator feels; his tone suggests that he desperately wanted to be with her and that he doesn't care how their togetherness will come about because he will do anything she asks. Similarly, from the phrase 'bound to obey' the reader can infer that he needs the woman to direct him through life due to the fact that he would be lost without her.

'Bare boughs overspread' conveys an image of entwining branches and togetherness, and the word 'Bare', linked to 'bare-browed' highlights the nakedness or vulnerability which is present. There is an interesting homophonic quality to 'bough' meaning branch, because it sounds exactly like 'bow', which has connotations of submission and deference.

Hardy then says he will leave her, as he followed her on, drawn to her by the narrow alley of trees. He repeatedly contradicts himself, confused between lust and responsibility. The bare boughs and branches of the trees were spread over above their heads, tangling with one another, creating a passageway. Hardy was aware he had to leave her to return home, but he couldn't overcome the passion that engulfed him. Fate could have turned them against one another, but it didn't, suggesting they are meant to be together, the key word at the end of the poem.

Hardy uses interesting adjectives to express his feelings of love and excitement. For example he uses colour to describe her cheeks. He uses the word 'crimson' to express passion. 'Crimson' is a deep red associated with love and lust and thus reflects the strength of feeling on display, albeit beneath the surface.

No Buyers: A Street Scene

A load of brushes and baskets and cradles and chairs
Labours along the street in the rain:
With it a man, a woman, a pony with whiteybrown hairs –
The man foots in front of the horse with a shambling sway
At a slower tread than a funeral train,
While to a dirge-like tune he chants his wares,
Swinging a Turk's–head brush (in a drum-major's way
When the bandsmen march and play).

A yard from the back of the man is the whiteybrown pony's
nose:
He mirrors his master in every item of pace and pose:
He stops when the man stops, without being told,
And seems to be eased by a pause; too plainly he's old,
Indeed, not strength enough shows
To steer the disjointed wagon straight,
Which wriggles left and right in a rambling line,
Deflected thus by its own warp and weight,
And pushing the pony with it in each incline.

The woman walks on the pavement verge,
Parallel to the man:
She wears an apron white and wide in span,
And carries a like Turk's-head, but more in nursing-wise:
Now and then she joins in his dirge,
But as if her thoughts were on distant things,
The rain clams her apron till it clings. –
So, step by step, they move with their merchandise,
And nobody buys.

Commentary

No Buyers: A Street Scene paints a dismal picture. The first line foregrounds the wares for sale as though they overshadow, both literally and symbolically, the couple and their horse. The use of polysyndetic listing (with its repetition of 'and') adds to the feeling that the items dominate and that Hardy wants to project an unnatural and cluttered image. The subsequent use of asyndetic listing (without an 'and') is used to lump the man, woman and pony together as though of secondary importance to individual goods for sale.

The man and woman tread wearily beside their wares and appear to be subservient to, or at the very least dependent on, the domestic items they are trying to sell.

The melancholy tone of the poem is created by references to the rain (pathetic fallacy being a common device in Hardy's poems), the reference to a funeral tread, his dirge (a sombre song or lament), the pony being too old and weak to steer the disjointed wagon, and their lack of success. The irregular rhyme scheme gives it an awkward, shuffling gait and the shortness of the last line emphasises their lack of success.

On the Departure Platform Publ. 1901

We kissed at the barrier; and passing through
She left me, and moment by moment got
Smaller and smaller, until to my view
She was but a spot;

A wee white spot of muslin fluff
That down the diminishing platform bore
Through hustling crowds of gentle and rough
To the carriage door.

Under the lamplight's fitful glowers,
Behind dark groups from far and near,
Whose interests were apart from ours,
She would disappear,

Then show again, till I ceased to see
That flexible form, that nebulous white;
And she who was more than my life to me
Had vanished quite ...

We have penned new plans since that fair fond day,
And in season she will appear again –
Perhaps in the same soft white array –

But never as then!

- 'And why, young man, must eternally fly

A joy you'll repeat, if you love her well?'

--O friend, nought happens twice thus; why,

I cannot tell!

Commentary

On the Departure Platform is, according to one critic, an unmistakeably Hardeian lament on the irreversibility of time published before the death of Emma. It is a six quatrain narrative poem with a regular ABAB rhyme scheme and gives a dramatized and very visual account of a woman leaving the narrator to board a train. Although the narrator is very much in love with the woman, he feels that she can appear 'But never as then! The title brings an image of an end or leaving and the speaker simply says, 'We kissed at the barrier.' This sets the tone of the piece, and the lack of detail about the kiss suggests that it is quick and disconnected. The use of enjambment, such as 'passing through / She left me, emphasises sense of detachment. It is also worth noting that as becomes 'but a spot' the lines in the first verse become shorter as though visually becoming distant. The speaker does not mention their relationship or past moments, only the aspect of leaving; which is immediately determined by the reader as a negative.

The woman's leaving presence becomes "smaller and smaller, until his view of her becomes but a spot." This gives us the impression that even though she leaves, he is still waiting for her. The fact that he stands there to wait for her to disappear shows his wishful hope for her promised return. Images of her disappearing and "diminishing" into the "hustling crowds of gentle and rough" gives us a feeling that this may very well be the last time he will see her "to the carriage door." Hardy breaks the Victorian tradition as he portrays the waiting man and the leaving woman. As he watches her fade, not only does the woman fade from his physical and emotional self but also he places her in a point where she is going to become a memory that once was. This is further enforced by his depersonalization of her form, setting her as 'a spot of muslin fluff'.

Hardy choreographs the scene of a crowded train station with "Through hustling crowds of gentle and rough... [she leaves] To the carriage door". This gives us a sharp visual image of the chaotic nature of a train station and its inhabitants. People of all kinds "behind dark groups from far and near" with different directions and "[without] interests... apart from [theirs]" pass by randomly as their parting continues.

In the fourth stanza, the woman's return is further diminished as Hardy uses specific words to describe the man's account. Although "she would disappear, then show again" he will still "ceased to see" her heavenly appearance of "nebulous white" as she is "vanquish quite." It is clear in these lines that his hope to see her again is diminished and that he is rather heartsick. Hardy's use of words such as "ceased" and "vanquished" reinforces this concept. In this poem, it is always from the eyes of the man. In addition, we have no account of the woman looking back or having further attachments to the man, except for the departing kiss. The focus on just the man arguably shows the one-sidedness of the relationship between him and his partner. Once again, hanging on to the brink of hope, the character holds on to their promise of "new plans since that fair fond day" and believes she will appear again "in season." However, his uncertainty is obvious when he considers that "perhaps in the same manner... But never as then!" she would come back again.

The final stanza contains direct speech with an interrogative from a friend. The friend attempts to comfort the narrator and Hardy elegantly addresses the question as to why it will end as in 'eternally fly'. For some critics the question is self-contemplative, rather than a speech between him and a stranger. The answer Hardy gives is that the strength of feeling won't be felt "twice" and that he cannot predict what may happen in the "future." Uncertainty is a common theme portrayed in Hardy's work, and these last lines are yet another reoccurrence. It gives the reader the feeling that the narrator is rather uncertain about absolute love and is inclined to reflect on the changing nature of all things.

Neutral Tones Publ 1869

We stood by a pond that winter day,
And the sun was white, as though chidden of God,
And a few leaves lay on the starving sod;
-They had fallen from an ash, and were grey.

Your eyes on me were as eyes that rove
Over tedious riddles of years ago;
And some words played between us to and fro
On which lost the more by our love.

The smile on your mouth was the deadest thing
Alive enough to have strength to die;
And a grin of bitterness swept thereby
Like an ominous bird a-wing ...

Since then, keen lessons that love deceives,
And wrings with wrong, have shaped to me
Your face, and the God-curst sun, and a tree,
And a pond edged with greyish leaves.

Commentary

Neutral Tones, written in 1867 (when he was 27, and three years before he met Emma), is the most widely praised of his early poems. It is about the end of a relationship, and carries strong emotional appeal despite its 'neutral tones'. In the first stanza the scene and atmosphere is set, 'we stood by a pond that winter day'. No harsh sounds are present and the sentence epitomises the tranquillity yet disheartening nature of the poem. In the second line we get even more of these very 'neutral' monosyllabic words 'the sun was white, as though chidden of God' in this sentence the poets attempt to stay within his own themes are very explicit by the use of the adjective 'white' to describe the sun, the sun normally represented by the colour yellow and a symbol for happiness and life. The very dismal atmosphere is reinforced by the use of the alliteration of 'L' creating a lazy yet unsatisfying tone. The further sibilance of 'starving sod' creates a harsh sound, adding a further layer of hopelessness. The metaphor of the 'few leaves 'symbolises the end of an era, hinting towards the dying of life. Yet, it is not life that died, but love.

The next stanza explores deeper into the nature of their relationship: 'Your eyes on me were as eyes that rove over tedious riddles of years ago.' This can be interpreted to mean the couple repeat the same fights without progress, the insignificance of their communication exposed through the tired and morbid undertone seen in lines such as 'And some words played between us to and fro-'. This shows fundamental flaws in their communication, making a meaningful relationship seem impossible.

The first line of the third stanza, in describing her smile, contains a heart-wrenching oxymoron. Normally a facial gesture associated with happiness and joy, here it is described as 'the deadest thing'. This provokes strong emotion in the reader, as the cold causality of the gesture serves as reminder to the bitterness of the poem. This oxymoronic metaphor continues, having made an impression upon the reader; it is now described as only 'alive enough to have the strength to die'. This further enhances the emotional turmoil inside the reader, presenting a horrifying image of something that just has enough energy to die, without breaking 'neutral tone'. This is one of the reasons why this poem is so effective: distance and neutrality of its language serves as a perfect example of 'less is sometimes more'. Another interesting use of symbolism is the 'ominous bird a-wing', a possible prolepsis to the final stanza, the ominous bird representing his now shattered trust, against an almost paganistic suggestion in 'ominous'.

The fourth stanza is finally one of total despair; however this is done without breaking the neutral melancholic tone of the poem. The narrator begins using phrases like 'love deceives', indicating an inner pain and turmoil yet to heal. He goes on to say that he was 'shaped' by the 'wrings with wrong', this alliteration shows how much mental anguish he has been through and we get to almost share his pain. The poem ends as it began, using neutral monosyllabic words. The change in the character becomes obvious, instead of referring to the sun as 'white', he now refers to it as the 'God-curst sun', reflecting the character's emotions changing from sadness to anger. The final line 'And a pond edged with greyish leaves' echoes the pond the speaker recalls at the beginning.

The fact that the poem ends with 'a pond edged with grey leaves' makes it circuitous as it ends at the pond where the poem is set at the start. Also, the depressed mood of the poem reflects the pessimism shown by Hardy in much of his poetry work. This pessimism was caused by many things: the industrialisation of Britain which meant that the traditional way of life in his country roots were lost; the expansion of the British empire which he opposed; his unhappy first marriage; and his fear and dislike of change.

No early poem better illustrates this process of composition than *Neutral Tones* (1867). Quatrains of Hardy's own devising confer a traditional emphasis on a traditional theme: namely, the end of an affair. Hardy's sweetheart keeps an appointment with him only then to end their relationship:

We stood by a pond that winter day,
And the sun was white, as though chidden of God,
And a few leaves lay on the starving sod;
– They had fallen from an ash, and were gray.

The perception which informs this poem is that the natural world is unsympathetic to the poet's unhappiness at being rejected; it is for this reason that the tones of the landscape, against which the parting takes place, are neutral'; he indents the fourth line in order to draw attention to the gray ash-leaves by which he proposes to make his pessimistic point. For the lovelorn poet, this parting is not such a sweet sorrow.

Hardy associates his feelings of rejection with the details of his immediate surroundings; his sorrow at losing his loved one takes on the colours of the sky (white) and the ash-leaves (gray).

Through life, he takes with him two memories of this bitter experience: first, he remembers her face with its cold, playful eyes (tedious riddles) and its moribund smile (deadest thing); second, he remembers the colourlessness of the landscape which mirrors her dissipated enthusiasm for their relationship. The fourth/final quatrain:

Since then, keen lessons that love deceives,
And wrings with wrong, have shaped to me
Your face, and the God-curst sun, and a tree,
And a pond edged with grayish leaves

begins with an adverbial phrase (since then) which tells us that the poet has been engaged in painful retrospection. Hardy has looked back at the event recorded in the first three quatrains and come to the conclusion that it taught him a keen lesson: namely, that love deceives. An alternative title for this lyric might be Sombre Tones, for he reaches a sombre conclusion, not that individual lovers are necessarily deceivers, but that love itself is deceptive: that is, it promises more than it can deliver, offers much only to disappoint.

Every subsequent time that he has suffered romantic rejection, Hardy cannot help but recall the unsympathetic shades of that autumn day. The pictorial images (face, sun, pond, tree, leaves) have acquired a mnemonic force. They have become powerful agents of the feeling that human emotions are out of place in a non-human universe which, if not actively unsympathetic, is nevertheless indifferent to them. Hardy, then, is ultimately concerned to paint a canvas on which the tones are neutral: that is, they reflect the grayish indifference of the non-human landscape to the plight of the human lover.

Drummer Hodge Publ. 1899

They throw in Drummer Hodge, to rest
Uncoffined – just as found:
His landmark is a kopje-crest
That breaks the veldt around;
And foreign constellations west
Each night above his mound.

Young Hodge the Drummer never knew –
Fresh from his Wessex home –
The meaning of the broad Karoo,
The Bush, the dusty loam,
And why uprose to nightly view
Strange stars amid the gloam.

Yet portion of that unknown plain
Will Hodge for ever be;
His homely Northern breast and brain
Grow to some Southern tree,
And strange-eyed constellations reign
His stars eternally.

Hardy and the Boer War

Hardy, as a patriotic Englishman, did not disagree completely with Britain's policies, but he could not understand the triumphalism in some quarters at the prospect of another war. He was less concerned with the greater issues than the experiences of those fighting and dying thousands of miles from home. The husband of his close friend and confidant Florence Henniker was a major in the Coldstream Guards, and his communications with her betray Hardy's disenchantment: 'I constantly deplore the fact that 'civilised' nations have not learnt some more excellent and apostolic way of settling disputes than the old & barbarous one.'

Hardy had cycled to Southampton to see Buller and the troops off on their way. The emotions on the faces of the people on the ships and at the quayside — excitement mixed with foreboding - were captured in his poem The Departure (later titled Embarkation), published in the Daily Chronicle on 25 October 1899. His most memorable work, Drummer Hodge, concerns an unspectacular soldier, the victim of a conflict beyond his understanding, whose remains are valued as something precious by the landscape that has become his new home: 'His homely Northern breast and brain/ Grow to some Southern tree.' The unlamented Hodge is now part of a larger, cosmic picture, against which the war pales into insignificance. A Christmas Ghost-Story dates from the same period, and was published in the Westminster Gazette on 23 December. It is deliberately ambiguous; the ghost could be either a Boer or a Briton, and the underlying theme lead to Hardy being accused of pacifism by an apoplectic Daily Chronicle on, of all days, Christmas Day. The Souls of the Slain shows a commitment to ordinary, unheroic values. The ghosts of soldiers killed in battle return home to bask in the glory of their deeds, but are met by 'a senior soul-flame' who shows them that they are remembered for dearer things by their loved ones, not their sacrifice for Queen and country.

On a first reading of Drummer Hodge there are some questions that spring to mind:
Who are 'they' and what is their attitude to Hodge? The poem begins ambiguously. 'They' could refer to either friend or foe. Their identity is not as important as their attitude to their discovery. None of the funeral traditions are observed: Hodge is 'thrown' into a pit 'just as found', without a coffin and presumably without a service. Hodge is representative of the thousands of casualties of the battle, just one more unremarkable victim.

How did Hodge react to South Africa?

There is some mortal irony that Hodge gave his life for a country and cause of which he was largely ignorant. The poem makes constant reference to Hodge's lack of knowledge - the name Hodge is synonymous with country yokels. His 'homely Northern breast and brain' suggests Hodge was a simple, unpretentious sort, but a valuable human nonetheless. While alive Hodge never felt comfortable with the new and unfamiliar night sky, or had the time to learn the names of his new surroundings, yet this alien landscape becomes his permanent home. The constellations that were foreign to him become 'His stars eternally.'

What is the poem's form?

The poem is very structured, never deviating from its metre or abab form. The Roman numerals at the head of each stanza provide a classical feel to the poem. It is as if Hardy is paying his own tribute to the otherwise unlamented Hodge, treating him as with the deference that was lacking from his burial.

What is the poem about?

The poem is an existentialist paradox - Hodge was an unimportant figure in a major war, but becomes a vital part of something that will last far longer than any human conflict.

The opening lines concentrate on the waste of Hodge's death, the lack of mourning contrasting with the traditional glorification of the war dead. Hodge will never be a hero among men, but he is elevated to a divine level through the Southern landscape that harbours him as something precious.

Historical Context

Drummer Hodge was originally published under the title The Dead Drummer in the 25th November edition of Literature, weeks after the war began. It appeared at a time when Hardy was struggling to prove his worth as a poet. His first published collection, Wessex Poems was a selection of his work dating from the 1860's to the publishing date, came out in December 1898 and the reviews were mostly hostile. The furore caused by Jude the Obscure had affected his reputation and many of the influential critics were not prepared to accept Hardy the Poet. The criticism wounded Hardy, and his early poems of 1899 were deeply introspective. The outbreak of war gave him the subject matter and inspiration to make better use of his downbeat frame of mind when turning his attention to the story of a local boy killed in the early part of the war.

The drummer boy had long played a significant part in war literature. The dramatic appeal of a naive young lad becoming a man in dangerous circumstances stirred the emotions of many a writer. One of the more recent had been Kipling's short story, The Drums of the Fore & Aft, where two grubby, drunken tykes inspire a great victory in India through their pluck and daring. Hardy's decision to cast Hodge as a drummer was a deliberate attempt to debunk the mythology that surrounded war-glory by showing one of the staple characters in a pathetic light.

It had only been in recent years that soldiering had been regarded as anything other than a profession for the lowest in society, a fate only slightly better than prison. Far-reaching reforms had created a more democratic army, popular with the general public. As the British soldier became humanised, the roguery that had seen him despised became part of his charm. Tales of heroic deeds in far-flung countries by Kipling and Rider Haggard sold in great volume. The growing pacifist movement of the 19th century looked upon the ordinary soldier as a victim of other men's cruelty. While other poets wrote of the sights and smells of the battle, Hardy concentrates on the aftermath, pointing out the broken body of Hodge, lying almost unnoticed, a victim of a madness that should have been dispensed with years before.

A first read reveals that Hodge is a youngster from Wessex who had only been in this foreign land (the South African karoo) for a short time before he died. He was a drummer. His body is found and is buried in this foreign land where he died. Although not apparent from the poem itself, the historical context tells us that

Hardy is writing about the Boer War which took place in South Africa at about the end of the nineteenth and start of the twentieth centuries. The Boers were the Dutch farmers who had been in occupation since the mid 1600's and who were rebelling against English rule in South Africa.

Line 1 word 2: 'throw' - a verb that sets the tone of the entire piece and sums up the attitude which the poet wishes to convey. The body is thrown, carelessly, unceremoniously, into a hole. There is no coffin. This is a hasty burial and it's unremarkable, unexceptional. We don't know from the poem who the 'they' are who find the body in the field. Given the nature of and haste of the burial, it is likely that he is found by strangers who happen upon the body, and not by comrades who were out looking specifically for him. If that is so, why is he called Hodge? The dictionary shows that hodge means a farm labourer or rustic. The word has lost the meaning it had in Hardy's day but then it meant any average worker. This isn't a particular fallen soldier - it is an average, general soldier.

Capturing Foreignness

Stanzas 1 and 2 are devoted to conveying the foreignness of the place to Hodge, assisted by the employment of the South African vernacular in places. Hodge was there for such a short time that he did not get to become familiar with his surroundings. S3 takes a sudden turn, however. It starts with the word 'Yet' and tells us that though the place is unfamiliar and unknown to Hodge, now that he is buried there a part of the plain will forever be Hodge. He will nourish an African tree and the southern constellations will west over him forever. Hodge becomes a part of the Karoo in which he died. The Karoo is forever marked by its past. While I'm not sure that one should make too much of the point - in death he becomes integrated with the landscape in a way that he did not in life.

History also tells us that the drummers of that time were frequently very young boys who often had never travelled far from home before. Their role was an extremely important one. The drum was used as the battlefield communication device, setting the cadence for the march and telling troops when to advance, retreat and regroup. Notwithstanding the importance of the role which the drummer held in the battle, this particular drummer is buried without ceremony and without anything to mark the spot or commemorate him. All that marks that he was there is the landscape itself.

So if that is what Hardy was wanting to convey, how does he employ the structure of the poem to assist in conveying this? Firstly, notice the meter. It is an alternating scheme of iambic tetrameter and iambic trimeter. These lines are short - like Drummer Hodge's life. It is rhythmic and metricated like the cadence of a drum, or of boots marching. Note also how the end-stopped rhymes are masculine - the stressed syllables of the words rhyme with each other. This adds to the metric effect and creates a resonating accent as one reads and a pause of each rhyme. It also integrates the lines very closely with each other. Note also how in S1 and S3 there is the use of the possessive personal pronoun 'his'. Mounds, landmarks and stars are all said to be his. By the use of words like Kopje and Karoo and Southern he places the scene geographically. By the use of the words young, drummer, Hodge and Northern breast he tells us a fair amount about the main character of the poem.

The strangeness or otherness of the place in which Hodge finds himself is conveyed using words like 'fresh', 'foreign', 'strange' etc and the feelings towards the place conveyed by using the word 'home' twice, once as a noun and once as an adjective. In such a short piece, note the number of times words conveying otherness or foreignness or strangeness are used. They far overwhelm the number of words describing England, South Africa, the war or the drummer.

This economical and very restrained poem contains no explicit (clearly stated) condemnation of war, but the implied criticism can hardly be missed. The language of the poem is for the most part simple and natural and conveys with clarity what befalls Hodge.

Drummers were usually the very youngest of soldiers, considered too young to fight. This drummer has a name that was once used as a kind of nickname or disrespectful term for people from the country (like 'bumpkin' or 'yokel'). Hardy does not support this kind of prejudice, and intends no ridicule here.

The poem tells of a West Country boy, who has fallen in battle in South Africa, during the Boer War. The strangeness of the terrain, of the soil even, and of the constellations that nightly appear over Hodge's grave is repeatedly stressed. Hardy uses Afrikaans words to emphasize this strangeness. The poem is restrained but evokes great sympathy for Hodge. From clues that Hardy works skilfully into the verse account we can work out a great amount of information about what has happened.

Stanza 1

'They' are not identified but are evidently Hodge's fellow soldiers, members of a burial detail. The use of the monosyllabic pronoun is most economical. Hodge is thrown, not lowered with dignity and military honours, into his grave. He is not even placed in a coffin (there is no time, or inclination from his superiors, to find one) and he is buried 'just as found' (a phrase better suited to an object than a person). It as if his body has not even been properly laid out, a suggestion confirmed by his being thrown into the ground. Hodge is given no headstone to mark the site of his burial, and the only landmark to show the position of his grave is the 'kopje crest/That breaks the veldt around' . The foreignness, to Hodge, of his resting place is emphasised by the use of Afrikaans terms such as 'kopje' and 'veldt' , and by the strangeness, to him, of the stars that rise nightly over his grave. The reference to the stars recurs in the remaining stanzas of the poem, providing a kind of linking motif.

Stanza 2

The contrast between the simple English boy, 'Young Hodge the Drummer', fresh from his West Country home, and his remote and alien resting-place is further developed in the references to:

•   the 'Karoo' (another Afrikaans term),

•   the scrub and barren soil, and,

•   the foreign constellations which Hodge would have witnessed before his death, but too rarely for him to come to know them.

Stanza 3

Yet, despite his ignorance of his surroundings, Hodge will now be a part of the South African veldt forever. His remains will nourish the roots of 'some Southern tree'. This stanza, too, ends with a reference to the alien constellations, which will 'reign' forever over Hodge's grave.

The pathos of Hodge's fate is made more striking by the restrained manner in which Hardy relates his burial. The young man's innocence and youth make his premature death seem all the more wasteful.

Discussing the poem

• The subject of the poem is a teenager - does this make a difference to its effect on you?

• How does Hardy show the strangeness of the foreign land where Hodge is killed?

• What is interesting in Hardy's language in the poem?

• How does Hardy use references to the natural world to explain Hodge's situation?

• What do you think of this poem?

Things to comment on

• Hodge's name - to some a term for a country 'bumpkin', but not to Hardy, who is sympathetic.

• The details of Hodge's burial - is it dignified? What is missing?

- What we learn of the battle - for what strategic position is it fought? Why all the hurry in the burial?

- The shortness of Hodge's service before his death - his unfamiliarity with the country and its soil.

- The irony of Hodge's being a part of this alien land forever.

- The repeated references to the stars.

- The presence or absence of comment on war in itself in the poem.

- The economy of the poem - how much does Hardy manage to say in these eighteen lines?

- Rhyme and metre.

- What you think of the poem, and why?

The Darkling Thrush Publ. 1900

I leant upon a coppice gate
When Frost was spectre-grey
And Winter's dregs made desolate
The weakening eye of day.
The tangled bine-stems scored the sky
Like strings of broken lyres,
And all mankind that haunted nigh
Had sought their household fires.

The land's sharp feature seem to be
The Century's corpse outleant,
His crypt the cloudy canopy,
The wind his death-lament.
The ancient pulse of germ and birth
Was shrunken hard and dry,
And every spirit upon earth
Seemed fervourless as I.

At once a voice arose among
The bleak twigs overhead
In a full-hearted evensong
Of joy illimited;
An aged thrush, frail, gaunt, and small,
In blast-beruffled plume,
Had chosen thus to fling his soul

Upon the growing gloom.

So little cause for carolings
Of such ecstatic sound
Was written on terrestrial things
Afar or nigh around,
That I could think there trembled through
His happy good-night air
Some blessed Hope, whereof he knew
And I was unaware.

Commentary

It was the art-critic John Ruskin who – in Modern Painters III
(1856) – coined the term pathetic fallacy; he did so in order to
criticise the growing tendency of both artists and writers to
ascribe human emotions to non-human phenomena. It was, so
Ruskin argued, a fallacy to suggest (as Wordsworth and
Tennyson regularly did) that human feelings could seek and find
a sympathetic response in their natural surroundings; such
sentimentality, he explained, created —a falseness in our
impressions of external things. In The Darkling Thrush, Hardy's
aim is to test the impact of the pathetic fallacy upon his own
powers of poetic perception. In this poem, he reflects upon the
extent to which the atmosphere of his natural surroundings can
support the feelings being explored by the narrative voice.

Originally entitled The Century's End, 1900, the precise date on
which The Darkling Thrush was first published is of immense

significance: it appeared in The Times on 29th Dec 1900. It is an occasional poem; what is more, the occasion for which it has been written is the first day of the new century about which readers of The Times are very likely to be optimistic.

The setting for this poem is a Dorset landscape in the bleak mid-winter. The purpose of the first two octaves is to describe this hibernian landscape from which the sheer cold has driven all mankind' but the poet himself; in order to describe this desolate scenery, Hardy selects a number of sharp features which characterise the dark season. Foremost among these features are the cadaverous trees of the coppice: namely, the leafless trees whose skeletal outlines (bleak twigs) show black against the sky. Given the occasion for the poem, such scenic details keep suggesting to Hardy that the century which has just ended has physically died and is outleant in its crypt; extending this metaphor, Hardy imagines that the mournful sound of the wind is singing a dirge (a death-lament) for the corpse of the nineteenth century. Given this morbid background, it is no wonder that all other living souls have sought their household fires' and that the poet himself is fervourless: that is, without energy/bereft of enthusiasm for life itself.

The poem has an abab rhyme scheme and is written in octaves (an eight line verse). On this momentous occasion, the last hours of the old century, Hardy writes his reflections in the first person, 'I'. He is leaning on a gate in a little wood – it's traditionally a thinking pose, and the poem conveys his thoughts and feelings. The gate also suggests a doorway into a new place, the new century.

Every living creature seems as devoid of passion as Hardy is, almost as dead as the century. Suddenly a thrush's beautiful song breaks upon this grim cold scene, the 'growing gloom'. Hardy wonders whether the bird knows of some reason for hope of which he himself is ignorant.

'Darkling' means in darkness, or becoming dark, for Hardy can still see the landscape, and the sun is 'weakening' but not completely set.

There are plenty of heavy, gloomy 'g' sounds: 'gate', 'grey', 'dregs', and equally heavy 'd' sounds: 'dregs', 'desolate' and 'day'. Even day, which might be cheering, is described as 'desolate' and having a 'weakening eye' – that's to say, the sun is going down and giving out only a weak light. And a person with a weakening eye sounds old, with little power.

The second verse intensifies the poet's perception of the gloomy wintry landscape in a series of metaphors associated with death. The landscape seems like the corpse of the century and the century is personified which intensifies one's feeling that it is a real presence. The cloudy sky seems like the century's tomb; the winter wind like the century's death song. Any 'pulse'(throbbing heartbeat) of germination and birth is dead, hard and dry. As in the first stanza, the first six lines are concerned with the winter landscape and the end of the century. And as in the first stanza, the last two lines of the second stanza are concerned with men; every spirit on the planet seems to have become as 'fervourless' (lacking in passion and intensity) as the poet, as hard and dry as the shrunken pulses of germ and birth.

Hardy's poem uses a variety of literary techniques to emphasise his pessimism at the turn of the century and the bleakness of the winter. The poem follows Hardy's thoughts and feelings about the new century and it seems as if the thrush knows something about the new century which Hardy does not. The thrush's call is the only piece of joy which penetrates through the darkness and it is alluding to the fact that the new century will hold lots of joy for Hardy even though he is pessimistic.

Hardy writes it in the form of an ode, conventionally a lyric poem in the form of an address to a particular subject, often written in a lofty, elevated style giving it a formal tone. However, odes can be written in a more private, personal vein, as in the reflective way that Hardy writes this one. On this momentous occasion, the last hours of the old century, Hardy writes his reflections in the first person, 'I'. He is leaning on a gate in a little wood – it's traditionally a thinking pose, and the poem conveys his thoughts and feelings.

It's obvious, even from the eventual title, 'The Darkling Thrush', that Hardy was consciously using words with a long poetic history. 'Darkling' means in darkness, or becoming dark, for Hardy can still see the landscape, and the sun is 'weakening' but not completely set. The title must be shorthand for 'the thrush that sang as night was approaching.'

Context

The word 'darkling' has a tremendous history in poetry. The word itself goes back to the mid fifteenth century. Milton, in Paradise Lost Book III describes the nightingale: 'the wakeful Bird / Sings darkling, and in shadiest Covert hid / Tunes her nocturnal Note ...' Keats famously uses the word in his 'Ode to a Nightingale': 'Darkling, I listen ...'. Matthew Arnold, in 'Dover

Beach' writes about the 'darkling plain'. Not only this, but there is a long and famous tradition of poems about birds, the Keats already mentioned, and those by Cowper and Wordsworth. The next phrase with a considerable literary tradition is 'strings of broken lyres'. This harks back to the Romantic notion of an Aeolian lyre or wind harp. Coleridge, in the 'Ode to the Departing Year' addresses the 'Spirit who sweepest the wild harp of Time' referring to an Aeolian harp or lyre, a stringed instrument that is 'played' when the wind passes over its strings. Then, with 'Its crypt the cloudy canopy, / The wind its death-lament' Hardy alludes to Shelley's 'Ode to the West Wind'. Shelley writes 'thou dirge / of the dying year', 'dirge' meaning 'death lament'. Several other rather consciously poetic words such as 'full-hearted', 'ecstatic', hark back to Tennyson, Wordsworth and Keats. In other words, this poem has a resonance of past poets and their thoughts
and feelings on a similar subject; it makes specific allusions to these poets and poems; their echoes are part of its tradition. It's a bleak and depressing mid-winter landscape. Hardy insists on that. The only colour is a ghostly gray.

Close Reading

I leant upon a coppice gate, coppice - little wood of small trees When Frost was spectre-gray, spectre-gray – frost made the landscape as gray as a ghost And Winter's dregs made desolate dregs - left-over bits desolate – bleak/deserted/dismal/miserable The weakening eye of day. eye of day – the sun. 'Gray' is the only colour left in the 'darkling' daylight. The rhythm is regular iambic tetrameter alternated with iambic trimeter (8 syllables in a line, with the second line in each case having just 6 syllables); it's a ballad stanza rhythm. This regular rhythm, seems to have a slow, joyless effect. The pace is slow. These lines in the opening verse establish a lifeless wasteland.

Suddenly the poet's eye alights on a detail: the mess of tangled, dried-up stems of a summer flower, carving a line against the grey sky and reminding him of the broken strings of a musical instrument. The tangled bine-stems scored the sky bine-stems – dried out stems of bindweed Like strings of broken lyres, broken lyres – broken harps And all mankind that haunted nigh Had sought their household fires. The dead flower stems form a reminder of summer, making the winter seem harsher through contrast. The broken lyre underlines the absence of harmony and therefore perhaps of joy in his vision of life. Harsh sounds add to this impression: sounds such as 'scored' and 'sky', 'broken' and 'mankind'. Even the people who have gone home to the warmth of their fires seem to have assumed a ghostly quality, 'all mankind that haunted nigh'. The world is a bleak, colourless, cold place with a few reminders of the melody and warmth that have vanished.

The alliteration in this stanza, with 'century's corpse', 'crypt' and 'cloudy canopy' intensifies the atmosphere of gloom and deathliness, and the rhymes of 'birth' and 'earth' are negated by 'dry' and 'I'. Everything is seen in terms of death: 'sharp features' (of a dead body), 'century's corpse', 'crypt', 'death-lament', 'shrunken hard and dry', 'fervourless'. It seems that it is not just the death of the old century that Hardy is describing, but the death of the pulse of life that vitalises and energises him and other people, the death of hope.

At this nadir, 'At once a voice arose' and it's the voice of an old, frail, thin, scruffy-looking thrush. Not the nightingale of Miltonic and Romantic tradition, whose arrival in Spring brings rapture to the poet, but the ordinary indigenous song-thrush, or possibly a mistle thrush, and a bedraggled one at that. It is 'blast-beruffled'; it has survived the winter winds (the word blast has a long history going back at least one thousand years, indigenous, like the thrush). And from the depths of the winter winds with their 'death lament' it brings its beautiful song; three run-on lines take us at full tilt to its message: 'joy illimited' (unlimited). The very words with which Hardy introduces the song are lyrical, rhythmic, repetitive, like the thrush's song: 'At once a voice arose among/The bleak twigs overhead.' In perfect iambics, each prefaced by the vowel 'a', Hardy echoes the sound of the thrush's song: 'at once a voice arose among...'

The poet juxtaposes the opposites: the gloomy last evening of the century, 'the growing gloom,' and 'the bleak twigs overhead' are contrasted with 'fullhearted evensong', 'joy illimited', 'fling his soul'. The poet, together with everything else on earth, 'seemed fervourless'; now we get 'full-hearted' song. 'Evensong' is the evening service of worship of God. The idea of religious faith is continued in the last verse, with the thrush's 'carolings', reminiscent of Christmas carols, and the 'blessed Hope' – hope being one of the three great Christian virtues, faith, hope and charity (love). The broken lyre strings of the tangled binestems, the confusion and lack of harmony in the early part of the poem, are contrasted with the ecstatic sound of the thrush's song or 'carolings' and 'air' (tune), and the perception of Hope. The thrush itself is 'aged' and 'frail', perhaps facing its own imminent end, and yet it flings it soul ecstatically upon the darkening evening.

In the first three verses there is a definite pause at the end of the fourth line (two full stops, one semi colon) but in this last verse, filled with the sense of life and hope brought by the thrush's song, there is only one comma in the verse; the rest of the lines are run-on lines, bringing us to 'some blessed Hope.' The 'pulse' that in the second verse 'was shrunken hard and dry' is contrasted with the 'trembled through' of the melody of hope. The whole poem is built upon this contrast: the first two verses cold and gloomy, the second two verses containing unlooked-for melody, joy and hope. Hardy's mood is reflected through the landscape and the season; but he (like Wordsworth in 'The Prelude' of 1805) is ready to learn from nature; a scruffy thrush can teach him about hope.

The Convergence of the Twain - (Lines on the loss of the Titanic)
Publ 1915

In a solitude of the sea

Deep from human vanity,

And the Pride of Life that planned her, stilly couches she.

Steel chambers, late the pyres

Of her salamandrine fires,

Cold currents thrid, and turn to rhythmic tidal lyres.

Over the mirrors meant

To glass the opulent

The sea-worm crawls – grotesque, slimed, dumb, indifferent.

Jewels in joy designed

To ravish the sensuous mind

Lie lightless, all their sparkles bleared and black and blind.

Dim moon-eyed fishes near

Gaze at the gilded gear

And query: 'What does this vaingloriousness down here?'

Well: while was fashioning

This creature of cleaving wing,

The Immanent Will that stirs and urges everything

Prepared a sinister mate

For her – so gaily great –

A shape of Ice, for the time far and dissociate.

And as the smart ship grew

In stature, grace, and hue,

In shadowy silent distance grew the Iceberg too.

Alien they seemed to be:

No mortal eye could see

The intimate welding of their later history,

Or sign that they were bent

By paths coincident

On being anon twin halves of one august event,

Till the Spinner of the Years

Said 'Now!' And each one hears,

And consummation comes, and jars two hemispheres.

CONTEXT

The Convergence of the Twain, published in 1915, describes the sinking of the Titanic on 15 April 1912. The poem consists of eleven stanzas of three lines each, following the AAA rhyme pattern. Hardy was asked to write a poem to be read at a charity concert to raise funds in aid of the tragedy disaster fund.

One interpretation holds that Hardy's controversial poem contrasts the materialism and hubris of mankind with the integrity and beauty of nature. This is said to be done in an almost satirical manner given the absence of any compassion, or even reference, towards the loss of life that accompanied the ship's sinking. The reader might expect to see evidence of grief, a depiction of the chaos or an emotive telling of individual losses. However, Hardy's poem does not follow these unspoken expectations. Instead, the poem focuses on the ship and the iceberg and how the two came to converge.

Seen as the epitome of Britain's wealth and power, the Titanic was extravagantly decorated and supposedly unsinkable. Peter Childs describes the Titanic as 'full of Edwardian confidence but bound for disaster and it is this display of vanity and pride that Hardy sardonically highlights in the first five stanzas as he contrasts the ship's current position in the Atlantic to its glory days where no expense was spared. By juxtaposing expensive items like the 'jewels in joy designed' with their position now where they 'lie lightless, all their sparkles bleared and black and blind' (IV, 12), Hardy emphasises the waste of riches resulting from the Titanic's failure.

At the beginning of the sixth stanza, there is a definite shift where Hardy goes from looking at the ship's past and present to discussing the cause of the disaster, the collision of the ship and the iceberg. The pairing of the two or the idea of a pair is constructed before the poem even starts. In the title, 'Twain', the archaic word for 'two' is used, generating the idea of a pairing, with the most obvious pair being the ship and the iceberg. From the sixth stanza onwards, Hardy's lexis suggests that the 'convergence' of the two forces was predestined, an unavoidable event premeditated by some hidden, uncontrollable force which is indicated in phrases like 'The Immanent Will' (VI, 18) and 'the Spinner of Years' (XI, 31). The unspoken force Hardy suggests is nature, and the pairing of human technology and nature can be seen quite clearly in the poem with all the new technologies of humans set against the larger force of nature. Hardy discusses that whilst the Titanic was being built, nature too 'prepared a sinister mate' (VII, 19) and, in the next stanza, Hardy creates a sense of menace in the lines 'And as the smart ship grew/In stature, grace and hue/In shadowy silent distance grew the Iceberg too' (VIII, 22 – 24).

Whilst critic Chris Baldick claims Hardy's The Convergence of the Twain 'alludes to a philosophical stance' and that it 'carefully refrains from moralizing' , fellow critic Donald Davie claims the poem 'very markedly censures the vanity and luxury which created and inhabited the staterooms of the ocean liner' therefore suggesting Hardy does moralize.

The unspoken expectations of the poem are left unfulfilled because rather than give the reader comfort, someone to blame or emotive stories of passengers, Hardy leaves the reader with an overwhelming sense of insignificance as it depicts mankind's greatest creation being overcome by nature, showing that humans will always be subject to a nature indifferent to 'human vanity' (I, 2) and 'Pride of Life' (I, 3).

Task: Explore how Hardy conveys the loss of the Titanic. Refer to details in the poem in your answer.

ANALYSIS

The poem's major ideas concern the vessel, its state, and symbolic significance two years after the collision, and a speculation on how the iceberg came to converge with the ship. Hardy is very interested in affiliating the growth and fate of the iceberg and ship through the deification of nature and time. The first five stanzas of the poem concern the submerged ship itself, while the last six discuss its fate while afloat.

In the first five stanzas, Hardy's descriptions of the Titanic are consistently juxtaposed against the ship's present environment to emphasize the waste of money, technology, and craftsmanship. The furnaces of the ship, which contained 'salamandrine fires' (5), now have 'Cold currents thrid' (6) through them. Where there was once heat and life driving the engines of the ship, there is now coldness and death. A further juxtaposition within this second stanza is the use of the word 'pyre' (4), as it connotes funerals and death, while the use of 'salamandrine' insinuates a certain tenacity for life (as salamanders were said to live through fires) that could be associated with the Unsinkable Ship everyone believed the Titanic to be before accident.

Hardy further emphasizes the waste of the ship's magnificence by describing how useless the 'opulent mirrors' are to uncomprehending sea-worms that are 'grotesque, slimed, dumb, indifferent' (9). The jewels on board the ship, now at the ocean's floor, become 'lightless, all their sparkles bleared and black and blind' (12). The poet's use of multiple adjectives and alliteration intensifies the somber nature of these descriptions. The items that Hardy has chosen in his poem to embody the loss of the ship (the cold furnaces, bleared mirrors, and lightless jewels, rather than the loss of life) are indicative of his attitude towards the ship and what it stood for.

The Titanic was not simply a ship built to traverse the ocean; it was a symbol of the wealth, power, and industrialization of Britain during this time. The items which appear in Hardy's poem are representative of the power, wealth and vanity of the British nation. Hardy's discussion of these items, rather than the more glaring issues of death and human suffering normally associated with the loss of the ship, would seem to indicate his disdain for the pride and importance that his contemporaries placed upon scientific and technological progress.

Hardy's discussion of the Titanic shifts in stanza six to address the cause of the disaster. His use of enjambment between the sixth and seventh stanzas seems to be a technique employed to represent not only the coming together of the iceberg and ship in the poem, but also their literal collision. Hardy's use of deification for both nature and time in the last six stanzas contribute to the ominous and fated quality of the Titanic disaster. Hardy suggests that the Titanic converging with the iceberg was not a coincidence, but rather an event planned by an 'Immanent Will' (18) and 'The Spinner of the Years' (31); inferring the ship had been destined for destruction since its inception. The eighth stanza, perhaps the most ominous of the poem, outlines how the ship and iceberg grew to their completion concurrently, 'as the smart ship grew / In shadowy silent distance grew the Iceberg too' (22, 24). Hardy uses words such as 'mate' (19), 'intimate welding' (27), and 'consummation' (33) to emphasize the apparent predestination that these two behemoths seemed to have, and to imply a wedding or sexual union of those mighty opposites.

Although he does not indicate implicitly that he believes in the powers he names, Hardy weaves these deifications into the poem to create a desired effect. The powers are not portrayed as benevolent or merciful as the Christian God would be, but rather they are the cause of this disaster. It would seem that Hardy is telling his audience that humanity, no matter how progressive we may become, will always be at the whim of nature, which has no feeling or care. We are not able to rise above or control a monolith such as the sea regardless of how far our progress has taken us. Knowing the Titanic disaster then, according to Hardy, should be a constant and humbling reminder of humanity's fallibility.

Essay Writing

Explore the concerns Hardy explores through his description of the loss of the Titanic. Refer to details in the poem in your answer.

On the surface - an account of the sinking of the SS Titanic in 1912. The ship was the pride of its time, adorned with luxury and opulence. Its destruction was brought about by the collision with an iceberg.

Below the surface Thomas Hardy explores areas of deeper significance.

- the pride and arrogance of humanity, vs. nature

- the power of Nature,

- the relationship between humanity and nature and

- the tension between appearance and reality.

Paragraph 1 – Introduction If you are unsure use the wording of the task to provide a frame for your essay. 'On the surface this poem appears to be concerned with a fairly simple event…….'

Paragraph 2 Consider the poem's title. A consideration of the title perhaps gives us the first clues to a deeper understanding of the poem…'

Paragraph 3 Consider individual stanzas of the poem eg -'In stanza I the poet creates a contrast between the worlds of humanity and nature…' Consider techniques such as alliteration, and use of capital letters.

Paragraph 4 Continue to explore stanzas and techniques. 'In stanzas II and III the poet uses contrasting language to highlight the distance between mankind and nature…'

Paragraph 5 Consider techniques such as alliteration. 'Line three of stanza IV is important in that the sound quality reflects the meaning of the words…'

Paragraph 6 'Personification is used in stanza V to communicate the poet's message that…'

Paragraph 7 Consider the general effect of stanzas VI – IX. Look at techniques such as tone, contrast in word choice, punctuation, use of capitals, enjambment.

Paragraph 8 'The significance of line 3 of stanza X lies in the image of twin halves, implying that the ship and the iceberg are...'

Paragraph 9 'The final stanza of the poem uses direct speech to convey...'

Paragraph 10 Sum up finally how the surface meaning of the poem only hints at its deeper significance and how a close analysis of literary techniques has made this deeper significance clearer. If necessary go back to the wording of the task to provide you with language suitable for a conclusion.

The Going Publ.1914

Why did you give no hint that night

That quickly after the morrow's dawn,

And calmly, as if indifferent quite,

You would close your term here, up and be gone

Where I could not follow

With wing of swallow

To gain one glimpse of you ever anon!

Never to bid good-bye

Or lip me the softest call

Or utter a wish for a word, while I

Saw morning harden upon the wall,

Unmoved, unknowing

That your great going

Had place that moment, and altered all.

Why do you make me leave the house

And think for a breath it is you I see

At the end of the alley of bending boughs

Where so often at dusk you used to be;

Till in darkening dankness

The yawning blankness

Of the perspective sickens me!

You were she who abode

By those red-veined rocks far West,

You were the swan-necked one who rode

Along the beetling Beeny Crest,

And, reining nigh me,

Would muse and eye me,

While Life unrolled us its very best.

Why, then, latterly did we not speak,

Did we not think of those days long dead,

And ere your vanishing strive to seek

That time's renewal? We might have said,

'In this bright spring weather

We'll visit together

Those places that once we visited.'

Well, well! All's past amend,

Unchangeable. It must go

I seem but a dead man held on end

To sink down soon….. O you could not know

That such swift fleeing

No soul foreseeing –

Not even I – Would undo me so!

Commentary

Emma Hardy died on the morning of 27th November 1912. If we read it as an autobiographical poem it appears Hardy had not realised how ill she was and was shocked by her death. He and Emma had been estranged for some time, although they continued to live together at Max Gate. Perhaps this is why he'd not noticed her increasing frailty. Her death prompted an outpouring of autobiographical poems, of which 'The Going' is the first, and the first four verses are very much centred on 'you' (Emma): 'Why did you give no hint … that … You would close your term here!' In verse five the focus moves to 'we', and what, as a couple, they might have said and done. In the last verse, the focus moves to Hardy, the desolate widower, undone by his wife's sudden 'going'.

Hardy calls the poem 'The Going' but he largely avoids the word death. He refers to Emma's death as 'close your term here, up and be gone / Where I could not follow'; as 'your great going'; as 'blankness'; as 'your vanishing' , and as 'such swift fleeing'. He uses the word dead only twice. In the penultimate verse, he asks with remorse why they did not think of the happy days when they first met, 'those days long dead … and strive to seek / That time's renewal?' That hope has now died with Emma's death. The second time he uses the word dead is in the last verse, describing himself: 'I seem but a dead man.' This means that the emphasis of the poem falls on how different everything seems without her, 'and altered all'. She has gone where Hardy cannot follow, cannot ever see her again, cannot ever speak to her again. He keeps thinking that he sees her and finds nothing but 'darkening dankness' and 'yawning blankness' – emptiness. The suddenness of her departure is dwelt on: 'quickly', 'such swift fleeing' and Hardy's inability to get his mind round it.

The structure of the poem is unusual and the syllable count varies from 5 to 11.Verses 1, 3 and 5 all start with interrogative Why? 'Why did you give no hint that night…!' 'Why do you make me leave the house …!' 'Why then latterly did we not speak …?' In the first verse, the opening line runs on to the next, re-enacting 'that quickly after the morrow's dawn' Emma left this life. Then the third line slows, reflecting Emma's calm and indifference. The short lines detailing Hardy's desire to follow her, 'to gain one glimpse of you' and his inability to do so are run-on lines. Light, dark and time feature prominently in the first three verses. Is it that Emma has gone from the light of this world into the darkness, that is, the unknown, of the next? Or are all these mentions of light and dark, night, dawn, morning, more importantly awareness of time, together with words like 'while' and 'quickly after' and 'that moment'? Time that brings such unforeseen changes, time that alters everything. The change from life to death in the first two verses; the change from love to indifference in the fourth and fifth verses. Time that was not well used, in the fifth verse, with its attendant thoughts of all that might have been.

In each case, the verse crying out, 'Why did you!' 'Why do you!' 'Why, then, latterly did we not?' is followed by the differently structured verse containing reflections, feelings, memories. 'Why did you give no hint ...?' is followed by Hardy's reflection that Emma left with no good-bye and he, watching daylight lighting up the wall, knew nothing of what was happening to her upstairs in her attic bedroom. 'Why do you make me leave the house / And think for a breath it is you I see?' is followed by his vivid memory of her as she was in Cornwall in 1870 when they first met. 'Why, then, latterly did we not speak..?' is followed by the desolate realisation that nothing can be changed now: 'Well, well! All's past amend, / Unchangeable.' The poem insists on how absolute is the difference made by death. Again and again in the first two verses Hardy describes this. 'I could not follow ... ever anon' (ever again). Here the rhymed words play their part: 'dawn' (when Emma died), 'be gone' (a euphemism for death and a half rhyme with dawn), 'ever anon' (ever again). 'Never to .. or... or...altered all.' (Here the structure does the insisting: never.. or.. or.. followed by the assonance of 'altered all' and the finality of the stressed monosyllable 'all' at the end of the verse.)

In verses 3 and 4 Hardy thinks he can see Emma. First he thinks 'for a breath (a moment, and how ironic that he uses the word breath which is synonymous with life) it is you I see.' He thinks (and he moves into the present tense, to convey the immediacy of his impression) that he sees her at dusk 'at the end of the alley of bending boughs' and for some critics the enjambment mimics the bending boughs and make the reader peer through them wondering if Emma can be seen. She can't, and the short 5th and 6th lines and the short stressed monosyllable 'me' at the end of the verse make this irreversible. Next, Hardy sees Emma in memory in verse 4, the Emma he first knew. He repeats the phrase 'You were ..'. This is a beautiful and romanticised Emma in a romanticised landscape: 'swan-necked' (with a long graceful neck), 'who rode / Along the beetling (overhanging) Beeny Crest.' In all four verses, Emma has been in control. She left without giving any hint of her intention, she makes Hardy leave the house, she makes Hardy think that he can see her in the garden, she was the one riding along the cliffs who, 'reining nigh me, / Would muse and eye me', while he was the passive one.

Juxtaposed with the memories of Emma the beautiful, the penultimate verse considers what might have been with its repeated consecutive 'did we not'; 'did we not speak, / Did we not think...?' It adds ('did we not') 'strive to seek / That time's renewal?' This verse is full of verbs, full of the actions that they did not take, 'speak', 'think', 'strive to seek', 'might have said', 'visit together'. The word 'we' is repeated, followed by the phrase 'We'll visit together...'. This verse considers the togetherness they once shared and failed to rediscover, not taking the opportunities they had. And so to the sixth verse: 'Well, well! All's past amend, / Unchangeable. It must go.' The heavy cesuras bring the pace almost to a standstill. The half-finished sentences and faltering rhythm show the articulate Hardy unable to find words for his feelings:

'I seem but a dead man held on end / To sink down soon. ... O you could not know
That such swift fleeing / No soul foreseeing - / Not even I – would undo me so!

The sequence of poems Hardy wrote after Emma's death are elegies, the Greek-derived word for a lament for the dead. Elegies frequently offer an extended poetic consideration of the problem of death, but Hardy does not necessarily follow the conventional path. Critics have read the tone and feelings in the poem in different ways. Some detect irritation, almost a tone of squabbling 'Why did you give no hint …?' as well as grief and remorse. Some find anger and accusation, on the way through to guilt and tenderness.

The implication is that Hardy's love was renewed by regrets – not to mention Emma Hardy's written reminiscences… and his return to Cornwall in March 1913. Like George Eliot's Amos Barton, 'now he re-lived all their life together, with that terrible keenness of memory and imagination which bereavement gives'. There could be no pardon, he felt, for his inadequacy and the selfishness of his indifference in their later years. Regret and romantic memories mingled to create the inspiration …'

Context

Previous elegies, such as Tennyson's *In Memoriam*, had followed a conventional pattern which paralleled the normal processes of mourning and coming to terms with the loss of a loved one: shock at the person's death, followed by despair, resignation and finally reconciliation. The Poems of 1912-13 reflect this pattern but with significant variations. The early poems, like *The Going*, follow convention in that they record Hardy's shock at Emma's death and, in keeping with the elegiac tradition, also a refusal to believe she has died. *The Voice* is undoubtedly the bleakest poem of the sequence and it marks a return to despair and the creation of an ideal image of Emma, young, vital and warm in the core poems of the sequence set in Cornwall.

In Thomas Hardy Selected Poems Tim Armstrong writes: 'The first seven poems of the sequence express a sense of rupture (split, parting) and shock, a 'difference' between then and now.

They alternate between addressing her as 'you' and third-person recollections. Hardy models the opening of his sequence, 'The Going', on Coventry Patmore's 1877 volume of domestic elegies, 'To the Unknown Eros'.

Analysis of *The Going* By Jerry Curtis

Anyone who has ever lost a beloved wife or husband can relate to this sad, grief filled poem. Thomas Hardy's wife, Emma, died suddenly of an illness, and this 1912 first-person poem is all about him and his feelings. Some have even called this poem 'whining' and overly maudlin (Excessively Sentimental).

Maudlin or not, it is also almost a complaint where, even in the first line of the first stanza, he asks, 'Why did you give no hint that night / …(that) You would close your term here, up and be gone…'? Even if the reader knew nothing of Hardy's personal loss, one can see that this is all about dying. In the first stanza, again, the poet tells us that the object of this poem went 'Where I could not follow /… To gain one glimpse of you ever anon!'

In the second stanza, the poet tells of how his world has been altered permanently. Worse yet, he chides (Tell Somebody Off) her again for having 'Never to bid good-bye /…Or utter a wish for a word…' Yet, even as she died, the morning came to 'harden on the wall.' Little did he know that her 'great going / Had place that moment, and altered all.' In the third stanza, the poet ramps up his grief to almost a statement of blame or indictment. 'Why do you make me leave the house…?' the author complains, only to see 'The yawning blankness …' as he thinks 'for a breath' it is her he sees 'At the end of the alley of bending boughs.' This stanza reeks of dark gloom and self-pity that is nearly unbearable.

The author brightens up somewhat in stanza four as he reminds himself of his earlier days with his Emma when she was alive. She was, it seemed, seemingly immortal. She lived 'by those red-veined rocks far West,' and she was part of the 'very best' while 'Life unrolled' it.

Next, the poet states what every grieving person must feel remembering love's acquaintance becoming overly familiar as the original spark inevitably leaves a relationship. There is kind of a double-barreled grief there. It is the regret that they might have said 'of those days long dead' that 'In this bright spring weather' they might again visit 'Those places that once we visited.'

In the last stanza, though, the author accepts the 'unchangeable' change: '...All's past (beyond) amend.' If possible, though, he gets even gloomier. He tells Emma, 'I seem but a dead man held on end/To sink down soon...' But he again, castigates poor, mute Emma with a parting shot that reaches the zenith of his self-pity: '...O you could not know / That such swift fleeing /...would undo me so.'

In the final analysis, though, grief is more about those left behind than those who die, and are beyond the sense of loss that death brings. The poet, then, can probably be pardoned for an excess of self-pity. Maybe, however, he should not have been so tough on poor Emma. She was the one who got sick and died, after all.

Detailed commentary on *The Going* by Andrew Moore

Hardy asks Emma why she did not alert him to her imminent death, but left him 'as if indifferent quite' to his feelings, without bidding him farewell: neither softly speaking words of parting, nor even asking him to speak a last word to her. He notes how, as the day dawned, he was unaware of what was happening to his wife, and of how this 'altered all'.

Hardy asks Emma why she compels him to go outside, making him think, momentarily, that he sees her figure in the dusk, in the place where she used to stand, but ultimately distressing him as, in the gathering gloom, he sees only 'yawning blankness' and not the familiar figure of Emma.

Turning back to the days when Emma's youth and beauty captivated him, Hardy wonders why, in later years, the joys of their courtship were neither remembered nor revived. He imagines how they might have rekindled their love by revisiting the places where they met while courting.

Finally Hardy concedes that what has happened cannot be changed and that he is as good as dead, waiting for the end ('to sink down soon') and, in conclusion, informs Emma that she could not know how so sudden and unexpected a passing as hers could distress him as much as it has.

The metre of the poem is surprisingly lively, though the rhythm breaks down in the disjointed syntax and brief sentences of the final stanza. The brief rhyming couplet in the penultimate two lines of each stanza exaggerate this jauntiness, which seems rather inappropriate to the subject of the piece.

Though the reader sympathises with Hardy's evident grief, it is difficult not to be a little impatient with his tendency to wallow in self-pity. He reproaches Emma for leaving him, and thinks despairingly of his and her failure to rekindle, in later years, their youthful affection. Yet we feel that this is a tragedy largely of his own making. He has, after all, had some forty years in which to 'seek/That time's renewal'. The fact that he expresses regret at his failure to do so only when the possibility has been removed by Emma's death casts doubt upon the sincerity of his grief.

The Voice Publ.1914

Woman much missed, how you call to me, call to me,

Saying that now you are not as you were

When you had changed from the one who was all to me,

But as at first, when our day was fair.

Can it be you that I hear? Let me view you, then,

Standing as when I drew near to the town

Where you would wait for me: yes, as I knew you then,

Even to the original air-blue gown!

Or is it only the breeze, in its listlessness

Travelling across the wet mead to me here,

You being ever dissolved to existlessness,

Heard no more again far or near?

Thus I; faltering forward,

Leaves around me falling,

Wind oozing thin through the thorn from norward,

And the woman calling.

Commentary

The Voice is a melancholy poem expressing Hardy's grief at the death of his first wife with whom his relationship was somewhat less than satisfactory. It was only after her death that he realised her worth and poured out his feelings in a sequence of poems of regret.

The technical aspects of the poem support the ideas in that the somewhat knotty syntax of the first stanza captures Hardy's tortuous feelings about Emma. In the third stanza 'listlessness' and 'existlessness' echo the sound of the wind through the trees. And in the last stanza the lines become shorter as he falters forward, growing weaker and weaker in his sorrow.

The Voice gives of an air of pessimism and apparent helpless but not because of physical incapacity but instead of a personal conflict involving another. The speaker is almost haunted by the thought of his lover looking for him or her but no longer being the same person that she was before. The speaker is not completely confident of his or her own abilities because his or her own thoughts are too fixated on the effects of the person, classified as 'you' in the poem, and how they continue to afflict or confuse the speaker.

The repetition of the person calling to the speaker emphasizes significance of this action to the poem and also how incessant it is to the speaker. In the first stanza 'you' is almost stressed every time that it appears yet 'me' is not stressed, when reading this out loud it is evident that the speaker is more aware of the action of 'you' than his or her own. There is slight repetition in the closing lines of the first stanza with the 'w' sound and this sound is attached to words that reference time along with 'who,' these sounds together mark the idea that the 'you' in the poem that the speaker longs for is in the past or no longer exists.

The second stanza of the poem is more centred on the speaker and his own inquiries about 'you.' There is a repetition of you throughout the lines but what stands out is where 'yes' is stressed before and after a pause, the sound alone prepares for the exclamatory closing line of the stanza that highlights the speaker's ability to actually make statements of his or her own about 'you.' Also the rhyme scheme unites the 'then' giving emphasis to all this being long gone and also the rhyming of 'town' and 'gown' point out the physical ties that remain of 'you' but mark even more her absence.

The last two stanzas are the more drained stanzas that leave an empty feeling in the reader. The rhyming of lines 1 and 3 of the third stanza and the plethora of 's' creates a feeling of vast emptiness because they seem to just trail off. The rhyme scheme also leads to 'here' and 'near' popping out but although there are definitive physical locations, they mark how the speaker is confused as to where the woman is and where he or she stands. The final stanza continues this vein with a sense of indefinite movement but also has a powerful sound image in 'wind oozing' which is paradoxical because the ooze sound makes the wind seem flaccid or dead. This mood allows the poem to conclude the poem melancholically by repeating that the woman is calling but no action is defined.

Thomas Hardy was married twice - his first marriage, long and mostly unhappy, was to Emma Gifford. They married in 1874. Emma died in 1912, and in 1914 Hardy married his secretary, Florence Dugdale, who later became his biographer. Hardy died in 1928, aged 87. He had asked to be laid beside Emma, but his body was buried in Poet's Corner in Westminster Abbey. Only his heart was placed in Emma's grave - or was it? There is a curious story that his housekeeper placed the heart on the kitchen table, where his sister's cat seized it, and ran off into the nearby woods. In this version of events, a pig's heart was duly buried beside Emma.

As in *The Haunter* Hardy imagines Emma trying to communicate with him. The poem is in the first person, and Hardy is the speaker, imagining that Emma calls to him. She tells him that she is not the woman she had become after forty years of marriage, but has regained the beauty of her youth, of the time when her and Hardy's 'day was fair'.

Imagining he can indeed hear her, Hardy implores Emma to appear to him, in the place and wearing the same clothes that he associates with their early courtship. Hardy introduces, in the third stanza, the mocking fear that all he hears is the wind and that Emma's death has marked the end of her existence - that she has been 'dissolved' and will be 'heard no more'.

The lively anapaestic metre of the first three stanzas gives way, in the final stanza, to a less fluent rhythm, capturing the desolate mood of Hardy as he falters forward, while the leaves fall and the north wind blows, as Emma (if it is she) continues to call.

The poem begins optimistically with a hope that Emma is really addressing Hardy. But by the end, a belief or fear that the 'voice' is imaginary has replaced this hope. Though the vigorous anapaestic metre of the poem helps convey this initial hope, it proves unwieldy for Hardy, as is evident in the clumsy third stanza, where 'listlessness' rhymes with Hardy's unfortunate coinage (invented word) 'existlessness', and we find the gauche and repetitious phrase 'no more again' in the stanza's final line.

Nobody Comes Publ. 1925

Tree-leaves labour up and down,

And through them the fainting light

Succumbs to the crawl of night.

Outside in the road the telegraph wire

To the town from the darkening land

Intones to travellers like a spectral lyre

Swept by a spectral hand.

A car comes up, with lamps full-glare,

That flash upon a tree:

It has nothing to do with me,

And whangs along in a world of its own,

Leaving a blacker air;

And mute by the gate I stand again alone,

And nobody pulls up there.

Commentary

Like many of Hardy's reflective poems, *Nobody Comes* contains
a negative outlook and expresses the feeling of self-pity
throughout the two stanzas. They both follow the same rhyme
scheme of A-B-B-C-D-C-D. It was written 9th October 1924 and

was first published in Hardy's Human Shows, Far Phantasies, Songs, and Trifles (1925).

Michael Millgate's biography of Hardy provides some important information about the context of the poem: In the spring of 1923, a cancerous lump on Florence Hardy's throat was misdiagnosed as a swollen gland. However, in September 1924, Hardy's second wife of ten years went up to London, where she was operated upon by surgeon James Sherren On 1 October, the surgeon reported to Hardy that the operation had been a complete success, the entire tumour having been removed successfully. Florence would be free to return home after spending a few days recuperating at the Fitzroy Square nursing home.

Novelist and poet Thomas Hardy, aged 74 at the time he wrote the poem, had been married for ten years to Florence Dugdale, some thirty years his junior, but a noted children's author in her own right. Nine days after the operation, Henry Hardy, the poet's younger brother, was entrusted with the task of driving her home from London. The party did not arrive back in Dorchester until well after dark.

Millgate describes Hardy's mental state a week prior to the incident that precipitated the poem: May O'Rourke, arriving at Max Gate the morning of the operation, was shocked by Hardy's physical appearance, and even after the news of the operation's success had arrived he remained as if 'dazed'. He felt additional distress and some guilt at not being on hand in London itself, but Florence could only have been disturbed by his frail and fretful presence

Two elements of technology stand in close contrast to the emptiness of the organic world. The telegraph wire in the first stanza should be an image of progress, of globalization, of a new information economy. Instead it's a 'spectral lyre' haunted instrument that suggests nothing except a kind of eerie image of dissociation. (The telegraph, an invention of Hardy's youth). In the second stanza, the car (not a common sight on English roads till Hardy was an old man) comes up, but instead of bringing the speaker into closer contact with the rest of his community, it merely leaves ' blacker air': making the setting even lonelier by contrast to the brief impersonal light its shone on the surroundings.

During Wind and Rain Publ. 1913

They sing their dearest songs –

He, she, all of them - yea,

Treble and tenor and bass,

And one to play;

With the candles mooning each face......

Ah, no; the years O!

How the sick leaves reel down in throngs!

They clear the creeping moss –

Elders and juniors – aye,

Making the pathways neat

And the garden gay;

And they build a shady seat ...

Ah, no; the years, the years;

See, the white storm-birds wing across!

They are blithely breakfasting all –

Men and maidens – yea,

Under the summer tree,

With a glimpse of the bay,

While pet fowl come to the knee...

Ah, no; the years O!

And the rotten rose is ript from the wall.

They change to a high new house,

He, she, all of them – aye,

Clocks and carpets and chairs

On the lawn all day,

And the brightest things that are theirs...

Ah, no; the years, the years;

Down their carved names the rain-drop ploughs.

Commentary

Hardy, in a philosophical mood, accepts with equanimity the tragic irony of the human condition: namely, that finite man must find an attitude to support himself in an infinite universe. There is no more complete expression of this acceptance than During Wind and Rain. Following Emma's death, Hardy read some of her recollections of her early years in Plymouth and compounded them into this elegy for their brief lives. Both in its symmetrical form and in this theme, his elegy owes a great deal to Feste's song at the end of Twelfth Night:

They change to a high new house,
He, she, all of them –- aye,
Clocks and carpets and chairs
On the lawn all day,
And brightest things that are theirs ....
Ah no; the years, the years;

Down their carved names the rain-drop ploughs.

Hardy structures each of his four stanzas so that a moment from the ideal past is brought hard up against a moment from the real present: for example, the change to a high new house (9 Bedford Terrace, Plymouth) conflicts ironically with the change that the ploughing rain-drop makes to their head-stones. In order to persuade us that this ironic change is entirely typical, Hardy selects for each stanza simple details which are themselves typical of everyday life. In this way, he creates the solemn impression that there is nothing more to the business of human living than the swift reduction of our best endeavours to an eroded head-stone: the change to a new house then is nothing beside the change to the head-stone now. He isolates his cast of archetypal characters in their natural state of flux and thus demonstrates how rapidly the excitement that goes with moving house recedes in the vast perspective of time.

Finally, *During Wind and Rain* relies for its symbolism upon Feste's chorus: For the rain, it raineth every day' (Act V Scene 1). The poem trades upon the unsurprising fact that attitudes to time have altered little since that day when a mournful minstrel first coined for his folk-song the chorus-lines – Ah no; the years O! and Ah, no; the years, the years – which Hardy has borrowed. Douglas Brown remarks that these ballad-refrains —recollect the way men and women in all ages have found things to be||: in this case, they bear the burden of the realisation that wind and rain, themselves agents of erosion, are symbolic of the natural forces that wear away human existences. Life, according to Hardy, takes place during wind and rain.

Close Reading

The poem, first published in 1913, tells us how time robs us of our memories and how death could take away loved ones. It deals with the loss of Hardy's wife, Emma, and contrasts her death with her childhood. The poem consists of four seven-line stanzas with the first five about moments in Emma's life and the final two lines are dark images of death.

The second line of each stanza has a semi-refrain such as the lines: 'He, she, all of them – yea,' 'Elders and juniors – aye,' 'Men and maidens – yea,' and 'He, she, all of them – aye.' This helps to add impact to the images Hardy invokes in his reader's mind.

The poem starts with, 'They sing their dearest songs' and follows with four lines describing the happy scene. Hardy masterfully twists a pleasant image into mournful and yet still lyrical depiction of decay in the last line 'sick leaves reel down in throngs!'

The second stanza is about time looming above to ravish the beauty of life. The lines, 'They clear the creeping moss- / Elders and juniors-aye, / Making the pathways neat / And the garden gay; / And they build a shady seat....' help create an image of life flourishing. The poem next mentions 'the years' and leaves the reader with death waiting as 'the white storm-birds wing across!' In many of Hardy's poems time is death's tool.

The third stanza uses the sense of smell to convey the message of death. The first line of this stanza finds the family 'breakfasting.' In contrast, the last line, 'And the rotten rose is ripped from the wall' leaves the reader with the stench of death in their nose.

The last stanza tells how the family finally achieved success by saying 'They change to a high new house,' and Hardy goes on to express the lavishness of their life. Once again 'the years' rob the people in the poem. Ergo, the reader is left with the image of 'raindrops' coming down to 'carve[d]' the families' names on their tombstones. This is the darkest and most final image in the poem. It also brings the reader back to the last line of the first stanza that had the image of decay.

These dark images conveyed in *During Wind and Rain* are one reason that readers find Hardy's work depressing. Death by the way of time is the ultimate villain that the poet shows in his work; there is no escaping the cold hand of mortality. However, there is beauty to the words just as there is beauty to be found in life.

I Look into My Glass Publ. 1898

I look into my glass,
And view my wasting skin,
And say, 'Would God it came to pass
My heart had shrunk as thin!'

For then, I, undistrest
By hearts grown cold to me,
Could lonely wait my endless rest
With equanimity.

But Time, to make me grieve,
Part steals, lets part abide;
And shakes this fragile frame at eve
With throbbings of noontide.

Commentary

Here the ageing Hardy studies the effects of time upon human
identity: in particular, he highlights the tension between looking
('my wasting skin') and feeling (throbbings of noontide). The
situation for the poem is a look into a mirror which the poet
takes; it alarms him with the stark realisation that he has grown
physically old. But the sentiment in this poem is complex, for
Hardy – a man in his fifties – is not simply regretting the fact that
his skin is wrinkled; he is explaining that he could tolerate his
physical decline with equanimity' [= calm] if only he did not still
feel emotionally robust. If his heart had aged at the same rate as

his skin, then he could await his endless rest (a euphemism for death) without particular anguish. As things are, he has to endure an unresolved conflict between his physical frailty (fragile frame) and his emotional vigour (throbbing').

What controls this poem is the contrast between eve' and noontide': between the poet's decline into old age and his contradictory feeling that he is still in the prime of his life. Although he is in the evening of his life, Hardy's heart still throbs with a young man's passion. Emotionally, psychologically, he feels as if he is still at his peak; but he is honest enough to admit that he no longer has the physical capacity to act on his feelings: in other words, his physical appearance conditions his attitude towards himself, modifies his sense of personal identity. In this lyric, Hardy is struggling to reconcile the sprightly way he feels with the decrepit way he looks. He concludes that, if only he felt as old as he looks, then he would not be so troubled.

Hardy was 57 when he wrote this (probably in 1897). Gloomier than ever after negative criticism of his novel *Tess of the D'Urbervilles* in 1891 and of *Jude the Obscure* in 1895, he was estranged from his wife, though they lived in the same house, and his admiration of Florence Henniker was not reciprocated ('hearts grown cold to me'). The tone is reflective; the pace is slow except for the final two lines of passion. Hardy is both looking at his reflection in the mirror and painting in words an emotional self-portrait. The poem is thus very much focused on himself: 'my glass', 'my wasting skin', 'my heart', 'my endless rest.' The poem seems to be concerned with how appearance belies reality; how other people see him (his elderly appearance) and how he really feels (passionately). In the first verse, words to do with age predominate: 'wasting', 'shrunk', 'thin'. The contrast is made between physical appearance ('wasting skin') and feelings ('heart'). Instead of a quiet mind ('equanimity') he experiences 'throbbings of noontide'.

Hardy illustrates the intensity of his feelings in the first verse when he writes 'Would God it came to pass / My heart had shrunk as thin'. He bursts out, passionately, with 'Would God' (I wish to God that ...). In the second verse he expresses his distress, his pain at 'hearts grown cold to me'. In the third verse he explicitly describes how his heart throbs just as it did when he was a young man in his prime. He paints his prime as the 'noontide' or midday of his life which he now sees as being in its 'eve or evening. Again, as in 'Hap', Hardy uses the structure of a syllogism but he changes the order of the logical stages. A syllogism's structure is: if ... but ... therefore the answer / solution is .... In this poem Hardy structures it 'if only' ('Would God ...') ... For then......But.' As so often with Hardy, the ending stresses the lack of any solution. Time is personified in the last verse stressing its proactive part in Hardy's bitter experiences in a sudden proliferation of verbs. 'Time, to make me grieve, Part steals, lets part abide; / And shakes this fragile frame ...'

Hardy repeats the sense of 'shakes' in the last line 'throbbings' (passion) to stress what he feels. There is a clear contrast between 'eve' (old age) and 'noontide' (prime of life). The alliterated 'fragile frame' insists on the physical age which belies his youthful emotions. The penultimate line runs over into the last line, speeding up the pace – the emotions spill over. Actually, this is so in all three stanzas: line 3 always runs on into line 4. In the first stanza this marks the intensity of emotion; in the second it reflects the longed for equanimity, with no punctuation to interrupt the rest.

Hardy seems to depict himself as being a sufferer at others' hands. He wishes he were 'undistrest' so obviously he is distressed 'by hearts grown cold to me.' He expresses this feeling in the passive mood, putting himself in the position of the sufferer. The coldness of other people's hearts is emphasised by 'grown cold' making Hardy in the next line 'lonely' – the continued assonance showing the effect of this coldness upon him. He is also a sufferer at the hands of malevolent Time in verse three. 'Time, to make me grieve, / Part steals, lets part abide; / And shakes this fragile frame at eve...'

Assonance again ensures that we associate Hardy's 'grieve'(ing) with the robbery of Time 'steals' in his old age 'eve'. Internal rhyme and assonance help us to link another source of Hardy's pain: 'Time to make me grieve... shakes this ... frame.' The ms in 'Time', 'make me' and 'frame' help to make almost unconscious connections between the words and their meanings. The last line, with its passionate plosives, the double bs of 'throbbings' leaves us with Hardy's pain. The poem's verbs start in the present, move into the conditional in lines 3 – 8 (the 'if only' section), and return to the present. Hardy's pain is in the present: now.

In Time of 'The Breaking of Nations' Publ.1916

I

Only a man harrowing clods

In a slow silent walk

With an old horse that stumbles and nods

Half asleep as they stalk

II

Only thin smoke without flame

From the heaps of couch-grass;

Yet this will go onward the same

Though Dynasties pass.

III

Yonder a maid and her wight

Come whispering by:

War's annals will cloud into night

Ere their story die.

Summary

The sedate and reflective poem was written in response to a direct request from the editor of the 'Saturday Review' for something that would help to 'keep the torch alight in the black', this being during the darkest days of the First World War. The poem is short and simple, comprising three quatrains with an ABAB rhyme scheme.

Hardy's mind flipped back to August 1870 when he had been courting his wife-to-be Emma Lavinia Gifford at her home in north Cornwall. Hardy was struck by the image of a horse-drawn plough breaking the clods in the field below and related it to a chapter in the Book of Jeremiah (chapter 51) that refers to 'my battle axe and weapons of war' with which 'I will break in pieces the nations … the horse and his rider … man and woman … old and young …' This is the judgment of God against the evil kingdom of Babylon. Hardy therefore felt that the phrase 'The breaking of nations', as part of the title of his poem, fitted the bill for the much larger conflict that was being fought as he wrote the poem.

The poet is struck by the contrasts between the horrors of a war being fought not all that far away and the ongoing simplicity of rural life. At the time when nations are being broken what he witnesses is: 'Only a man harrowing clods / In a slow silent walk / With an old horse'.

In the second stanza, while fires rage abroad as farms and villages are destroyed, he sees: 'Only thin smoke without flame / From the heaps of couch-grass'. The contrasts lie between the forces of destruction and construction, death versus life. The weapons of war may break nations, but the weapons of peace break clods so that new crops can be grown. Fire can destroy livelihoods, but, by burning weeds, can create the conditions for livelihoods to be maintained. As Hardy says in the concluding lines of the second stanza, 'Yet this will go onward the same / Though Dynasties pass.'

The third stanza's reference to 'a maid and her wight' seems to refer to a couple other than himself and Emma (hence 'Yonder') but the 'story' is the same, namely of young love that will grow and lead to the birth of the next generation. The idea that, despite the wars that men fight, the basic operations of producing food and creating children will continue, come what may, was a regular theme in Hardy's works, including his novels. For example, in 'Far from the Madding Crowd' he expresses the view that although castle and church may decay, the barn will continue: 'The defence and salvation of the body by daily bread is still a study, a religion and a desire'. 'In Time of 'The Breaking of Nations'' is therefore a poem of hope for the future, in any age. He concludes the poem, with reference to the representative young couple, by stating that: 'War's annals will cloud into night / Ere their story die.'

Commentary

This poem was written in 1915 and published in the Saturday Review, in January 1916 (the middle
of the First World War). The title of the poem is a quotation from the Old Testament of the Bible. In it, the prophet Jeremiah writes (Chapter 51, verse 20) 'Thou (he means God) art my battle axe and weapons of war: for with thee will I break in pieces the nations, and with thee will I destroy kingdoms.' A much more

modern translation reads: 'You were my mace, a weapon of war. With you I crushed the nations, struck kingdoms down, with you crushed horse and rider, chariot and charioteer, with you crushed man and woman, old man and young, youth and maid, with you crushed shepherd and flock, ploughman and team, governors and nobles.'

Hardy's title for the poem thus means, in war time. But the verses from Jeremiah show that although all sorts of people, including country people such as the shepherd and his flock, the ploughman and his team of horses, are crushed and killed during war, their way of life continues while the great events of history are forgotten.

Years earlier, Hardy copied into his notebook a passage from Charles Reade: 'The ... history of Waterloo field is to be ploughed and sowed and reaped and mowed: yet once in a way these acts of husbandry were diversified with a great battle, where hosts decided the fate of empires. After that agriculture resumed its sullen sway.'

This is a famous and much-anthologised poem. In it, Hardy depicts the everyday, unexciting happenings that people take for granted: the man and his sleepy old horse harrowing the fields ready to sow seed; the burning of weeds, the young couple in love whispering to each other as they walk past. Yet these, he writes, are the events that will continue to take place when the apparently important matters, the wars and families of kings, have been forgotten.

The first verse is entirely devoted to unimportant country sights and actions, dismissed by the opening word as 'Only' ... The second stanza, too, begins, 'Only …. Whereas the first verse described the slow silent work of the man and his old horse, the second stanza describes agricultural routine for two lines and then sets it against the important events of history with 'Yet …' Again, in the third stanza, the archetypal characters of a girl and her lover are juxtaposed with, and implicitly contrasted with, the important events of history: war. The historical records of a year of war 'War's annals' will fade away before the love stories of men and women in succeeding generations die.

The first stanza is simply set out in ballad form, or in a 'folk measure' (Tim Armstrong). Perhaps the ballad form emphasises the simplicity and timelessness of these unimportant everyday countryside actions. A man and his horse are engaged in harrowing clods, breaking up large clods of earth to make a fine tilth. The long vowels and peaceful 'l' sounds make for a tranquil, unexciting scene. The stanza has no punctuation to interrupt it; this, like other farming duties, is carried out year after year, for long hours each day. 'Only' starts a succession of long vowels on the 'o' sound: 'only', 'slow', 'old; then there are the frequent peaceful 'l' sounds in 'only', 'clods', 'slow', 'silent', 'old', 'asleep'. Often these ls are coupled with 's' sounds, 'slow' 'silent' 'asleep'. The whole effect is quiet, uneventful, nothing special. The figures are anonymous, 'a man', 'an old horse.' The horse isn't even a smart thoroughbred, just an old farm horse that 'stumbles and nods/Half asleep.' The stanza doesn't have a finite verb, it's as if the main clause got left out, and you're left with a subordinate (ie less important) clause: 'only a man… with an old horse …' And other verbs are hardly very world-changing: 'harrowing', 'stumbles', 'nods', 'stalk'. They're easy to overlook.

In stanza two, the dismissive opening 'Only …' is repeated. The smoke from the weeds ('heaps of couch-grass') isn't even conspicuous, it's only 'thin', and it's 'without flame'. The first two lines of the stanza don't even have a verb. This time a reflection, a comment, is introduced in the 3rd and 4th line of the stanza. The first two lines have been brought to a halt with a semi-colon to introduce the word 'Yet'. Burning couch-grass is only an unimportant farming activity, 'Yet… this will go onward…, though dynasties (ruling families) pass' into oblivion. The long slow vowel of 'o' is sustained through the first three lines of the stanza: 'only', 'smoke', 'go'. The rhyme of 'couchgrass' with 'pass' highlights the point that insignificant heaps of couch-grass smoking thinly will continue after the important dynasties have passed. The verb tense in 'will go onward' is future – it will continue. The 'dynasties pass' in the present tense.

In the third stanza, Hardy describes a young woman and her lover whispering to each other. Their story of love will continue when the documents of a year of war have long faded into oblivion. The sounds in the 'maid and her wight' are sounds that can be picked up from much earlier in the poem. The long 'a' vowel of maid was introduced earlier in the poem, with flame' and 'same'. The ds from the first stanza 'clods', 'nods', are continued through the second in 'dynasties' and into the third with 'maid' leading us to the d of 'die'. The long 'i' sounds that started in the first stanza with 'silent', continue into the third stanza take us to the same destination, 'wight', 'by', 'night', 'die'. 'Die', the important last monosyllable of the poem, insists that it is the story of the lovers and the tedious everyday farm jobs that will endure. The lovers' story long outlasts the world-shattering and oh-so-important events of History. Wight is a deliberately archaic word that Hardy uses here, as is 'Ere' meaning before -

almost suggesting that they are archetypal characters from a ballad, from
as long ago as there are ballads to chronicle their existence. There is a brief rivalry in the 'w' of 'wight' and 'whispering' with 'war' but the lovers' is the story that lasts. The maid and her wight come whispering by in the present continuous tense (like the man 'harrowing clods'). Again, war's annals will be over and done with (in the future) before 'their story die' conditional present tense continues.

We have in this apparently simple poem three rural vignettes (little pictures) juxtaposed in the second and third stanzas with mention of momentous events, 'Dynasties', 'War's annals'. Their importance is emphasised by their conspicuously Latin derivation and capital letters, all the more noticeable in their appearance within such short simple lines, ballad form, straightforward uneducated occupations. Yet in the first and second stanzas, where the rural occupations are introduced dismissively with 'Only', the second part of each stanza makes a clear assertion: 'this will go onward the same' and 'War's annals will cloud (pass) into night'. Perhaps even the apparently simple innocuous ballad form, so appropriate for the farming jobs, is not to be dismissed too easily. The almost inaudible conversation of the 'maid and her wight' (suggested by the slight sibilance of the s in whispering) is nothing beside the deafening noise of the war. But It Is the love story that will endure

Tom Paulin writes of this poem: the ballad states 'there will always be love and war.' Conspicuously educated, Latinate words like 'dynasties' and 'annals' suggest that there is a version of history that deals with Great Events. There are also the lives of ordinary people who will never appear in the history books, yet who will be there when the Great Historical Events are over and forgotten. Tom Paulin adds that the Roman numerals I, II and III are 'quietly and unobtrusively monumental' that is to say, important.

The Pine Planters

I

We work here together

In blast and breeze;

He fills the earth in,

I hold the trees.

He does not notice

That what I do

Keeps me from moving

And chills me through.

He has seen one fairer

I feel by his eye,

Which skims me as though

I were not by.

And since she passed here

He scarce has known

But that the woodland

Holds him alone.

I have worked here with him

Since morning shine,

He busy with his thoughts

And I with mine.

I have helped him so many,

So many days,

But never win any

Small word of praise!

Shall I not sigh to him

That I work on

Glad to be nigh to him

Though hope is gone?

Nay, though he never

Knew love like mine,

I'll bear it ever

And make no sign!

II

From the bundle at hand here

I take each tree,

And set it to stand, here

Always to be;

When, in a second,

As if from fear

Of Life unreckoned

Beginning here,

It starts a sighing

Through day and night,

Though while there lying

'Twas voiceless quite.

It will sigh in the morning

Will sigh at noon,

At the winter's warning,

In wafts of June;

Grieving that never

Kind Fate decreed

It should for ever

Remain a seed,

And shun the welter

Of things without,

Unneeding shelter

From storm and drought.

Thus, all unknowing

For whom or what

We set it growing

In this bleak spot,

It still will grieve here

Throughout its time,

Unable to leave here,

Or change its clime:

Or tell the story

Of us today

When, halt and hoary,

We pass away.

Commentary

In most cases it is possible to keep the voices in Hardy's fiction apart from those in his poetry, but there are instances in which Hardy revives some of his fictional characters. *The Pine Planters* is subtitled *Marty South Reverie* and is narrated from Marty's perspective. In the poem Marty expresses the feelings she had during the pine planting episode in chapter eight of Hardy's novel *The Woodlanders*. The Pine Planters therefore adds an emotional dimension to the episode in the novel, giving the reader an insight into Marty's feelings. Marty South, in *The*

Woodlanders, is a courageous peasant girl who, despite being the perfect mate for him, has been overlooked by Giles Winterborne. She is the only one to mourn his death.

Below is the relevant passage taken from Hardy's novel *The Woodlanders* (1886-87). Marty South is a plain and uneducated girl who falls in love with her work partner, Giles Winterborne. Her love is unrequited.

The Woodlanders (Chapter 8)

"Why didn't you come, Mr. Winterborne?" she said. "I've been waiting there hours and hours, and at last I thought I must try to find you."

"Bless my soul, I'd quite forgot," said Giles.

What he had forgotten was that there was a thousand young fir-trees to be planted in a neighbouring spot which had been cleared by the wood-cutters, and that he had arranged to plant them with his own hands. He had a marvellous power of making trees grow. Although he would seem to shovel in the earth quite carelessly, there was a sort of sympathy between himself and the fir, oak, or beech that he was operating on, so that the roots took hold of the soil in a few days. When, on the other hand, any of the journeymen planted, although they seemed to go through an identically similar process, one quarter of the trees would die away during the ensuing August.

Hence Winterborne found delight in the work even when, as at present, he contracted to do it on portions of the woodland in which he had no personal interest. Marty, who turned her hand to anything, was usually the one who performed the part of keeping the trees in a perpendicular position while he threw in the mould.

He accompanied her towards the spot, being stimulated yet further to proceed with the work by the knowledge that the ground was close to the way-side along which Grace must pass on her return from Hintock House.

"You've a cold in the head, Marty," he said, as they walked. "That comes of cutting off your hair."

"I suppose it do. Yes; I've three headaches going on in my head at the same time."

"Three headaches!"

"Yes, a rheumatic headache in my poll, a sick headache over my eyes, and a misery headache in the middle of my brain. However, I came out, for I thought you might be waiting and grumbling like anything if I was not there."

The holes were already dug, and they set to work. Winterborne's fingers were endowed with a gentle conjuror's touch in spreading the roots of each little tree, resulting in a sort of caress, under which the delicate fibres all laid themselves out in their proper directions for growth. He put most of these roots towards the south-west; for, he said, in forty years' time, when some great gale is blowing from that quarter, the trees will require the strongest holdfast on that side to stand against it and not fall.

"How they sigh directly we put 'em upright, though while they are lying down they don't sigh at all," said Marty.

"Do they?" said Giles. "I've never noticed it."

She erected one of the young pines into its hole, and held up her finger; the soft musical breathing instantly set in, which was not to cease night or day till the grown tree should be felled-- probably long after the two planters should be felled themselves.

"It seems to me," the girl continued, "as if they sigh because they are very sorry to begin life in earnest--just as we be."

"Just as we be?" He looked critically at her. "You ought not to feel like that, Marty."

Her only reply was turning to take up the next tree; and they planted on through a great part of the day, almost without another word. Winterborne's mind ran on his contemplated evening-party, his abstraction being such that he hardly was conscious of Marty's presence beside him. From the nature of their employment, in which he handled the spade and she merely held the tree, it followed that he got good exercise and she got none. But she was an heroic girl, and though her out-stretched hand was chill as a stone, and her cheeks blue, and her cold worse than ever, she would not complain while he was disposed to continue work.

ACTIVITIES AND TASKS

• A good way to learn things for an exam is to prepare a live talk for a specific audience, and then present the talk. Do this individually, in pairs or a small group.

• Write a script for a radio or TV arts magazine feature on Thomas Hardy. Record it (as well as you can). Play it back to your friends or yourself for revision.

• Prepare detailed readings (explanations, comment, comparison and evaluation) of poems or parts of them. Record these and play them back for revision.

Varying the audience

Prepare (for reading or listening) different kinds of text which show your understanding of the poems, which are suited to a range of possible readers or audiences. Some examples include:

• Teaching notes for people much younger or older than yourself

• A report to the Committee of the Nobel Prize for Literature (find out how writers qualify for this prize, and decide whether Thomas Hardy would have been a suitable candidate)

• A message to transmit to an alien

• An article for an encyclopedia of poetry (could be in print, on CD-ROM or a Web site)

• A letter to Thomas Hardy, explaining what you have enjoyed in reading his poetry

Imaginative writing

• Choose one or more of the people or characters about whom Hardy writes. Write a monologue (can be prose or verse) in which you speak as if you are that person.

• Use one or more of Hardy's poems as the starting point or plot for a narrative.

• Write a travel guide for the places you have encountered in Thomas Hardy's poems. Research with print and electronic media to find out more about them - show how they are important in his poems.

English Literature Exam

In the IGCSE exam you have 45minutes to answer one question. Below are questions for you to consider.

1   How does Hardy make the setting so vivid in *Drummer Hodge* AND one other Hardy poem you have studied?

2   What are your feelings about the ways in which Hardy portrays the relationships in *The Voice* OR *On the Departure Platform*?

3   How do you think the poet's words create a vivid feeling of sorrow in either *Neutral Tones* OR *The Voice*?

4   How does Thomas Hardy's description of a particular setting help to convey an idea or opinion? Explore in detail how the poems you have chosen make this idea or opinion vivid to the reader.

5   Explore the ways in which Hardy makes the narrative so compelling within *The Convergence of the Twain*

6   How does Hardy convey the feelings of his narrator in *The Darkling Thrush*?

GLOSSARY

Alliteration – several words starting with the same letter or sound, for example, 'bleared and black and blind'.

Assonance – same vowel sound in different words, for example, 'doped', 'sloped'.

Cesura – a break or pause in the middle of a line of poetry.

Consonance – same consonants in words that contain different vowel sounds, for example, 'bode', 'boughed'.

Enjambment or run-on lines – when there is no punctuation at the end of a line of verse and it runs straight on to the next line.

Onomatopoeia – the effect when the sound of a word reflects its meaning, like 'splash'.

Personification – when something that is not human is referred to as if it is a person, for example, the Titanic, 'still couches she'.

Repetition – repeated word or meaning.

Rhyme – very similar to assonance; same vowel sound and final consonant, for example, 'say', 'decay'. Masculine rhyme – when the final syllable is stress, as in 'say' and 'decay'. Feminine rhyme – when the final syllable is not stressed, as in 'growing', 'showing'.

Rhythm – the musical beat of the line, with stressed and unstressed syllables (the stressed syllables will be the important ones). The different rhythms have different names. Trochee (trochaic): strong light, strong light; iamb (iambic): light strong, light strong; dactyl: strong light light, strong light light; anapaest: light light strong, light light strong.

Then there are technical words for the number of lines in a verse or stanza.

Quatrain – four lines in a verse / Sestet – six line / Octave – eight lines.

Printed in Great Britain
by Amazon